ANDERSON ELEMENTARY LIBRARY SCHOOL

S0-AHA-359

SNAP SHOT™

Senior Editor
Mary Ling

Editor
Caroline Bingham

Art Editor
Joanna Pocock

Designer
Claire Penny

Production
Catherine Semark

Consultant
Phil Wilkinson

A SNAPSHOT™ BOOK

SNAPSHOT™ is an imprint of Covent Garden Books.
95 Madison Avenue
New York, NY 10016

Copyright © 1994 Covent Garden Books Ltd., London.
Picture credits: Cadw (Welsh Historical Monuments);
Royal Armouries / British Museum: 22 bl;
The Wallace Collection: 8, 16, 17tr, tl, bl, 18, 29bl

2 4 6 8 10 9 7 5 3 1

All rights reserved.

Every effort has been made to trace
the copyright holders and we apologize in
advance for any unintentional omissions. We
would be pleased to insert the appropriate
acknowledgment in any subsequent
edition of this publication.

ISBN 1-56458-730-4

Color reproduction by Colourscan
Printed and bound in Belgium by Proost

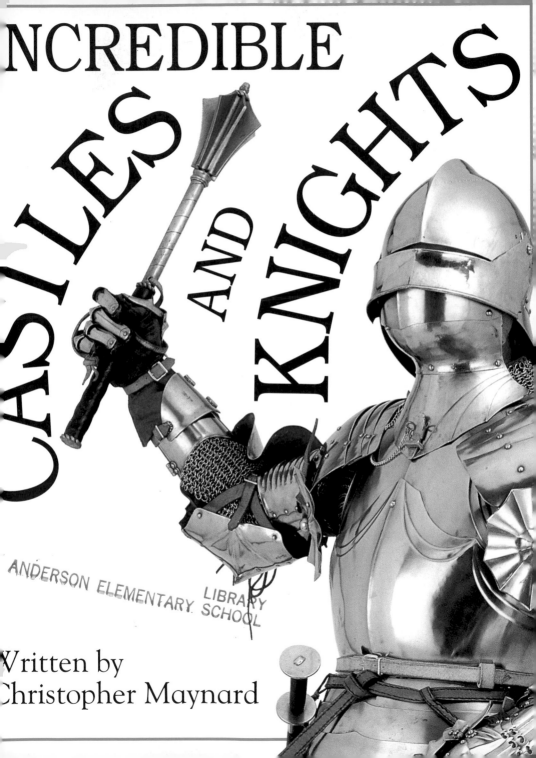

NCREDIBLE

CASTLES AND KNIGHTS

ANDERSON ELEMENTARY SCHOOL LIBRARY

Written by
Christopher Maynard

Lord of the manor

Contents

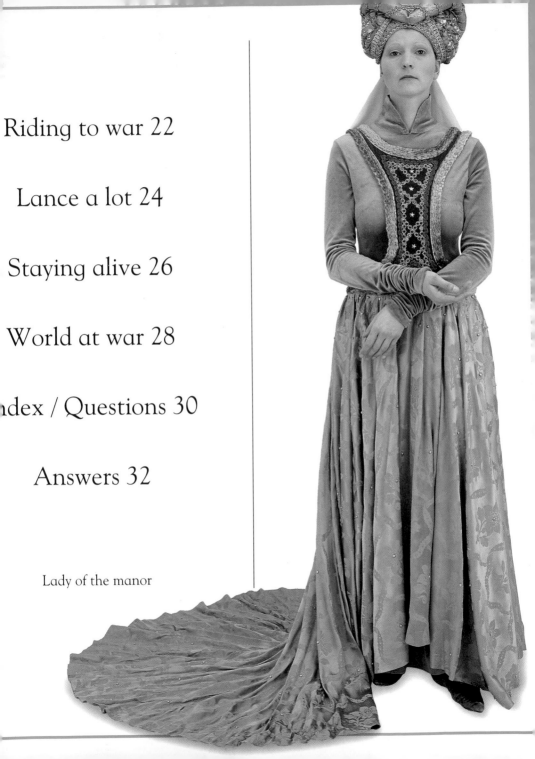

Lady of the manor

Castles and keep

During the Middle Ages, mar
rich and powerful lords lived i
mighty castles. A castle prote
its owner from bands of thieve
rival lords, and invaders from
other lands.

An iron-clad wooden portcullis was lowered over the door for extra security.

The slowest way to capture a castle

High towers, called turrets, gave a good view of the enemy's forces.

Soldiers could shoot out from slits in the walls.

In safekeeping

Early stone castles often consisted of just one tower, called a keep. They had incredibly thick walls, and might be 96 ft (35 m) high. Prisoners kept in the keep very rarely escaped!

ng to the top

main door was built on the second floor,
:ers had to force their way up a flight of
before they could try to break in.

s to starve out the people inside.

The castle gate was guarded by strong towers, a wooden drawbridge, and a portcullis.

The moat kept attackers from digging under the main walls.

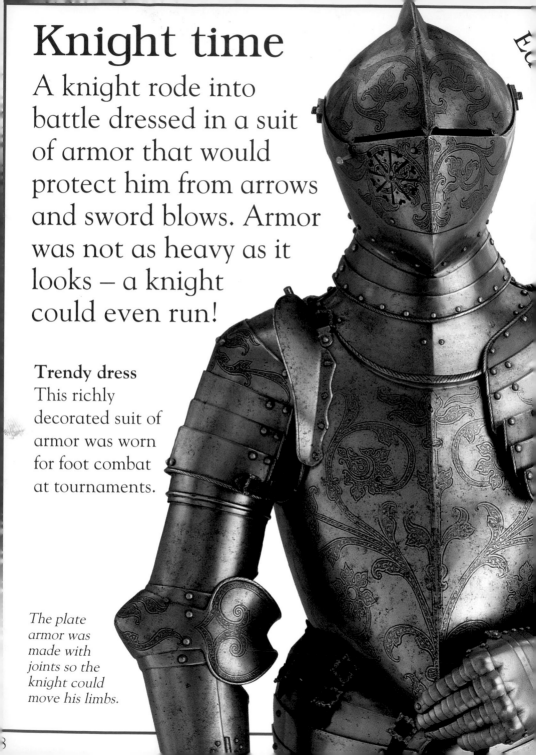

Knight time

A knight rode into battle dressed in a suit of armor that would protect him from arrows and sword blows. Armor was not as heavy as it looks – a knight could even run!

Trendy dress
This richly decorated suit of armor was worn for foot combat at tournaments.

The plate armor was made with joints so the knight could move his limbs.

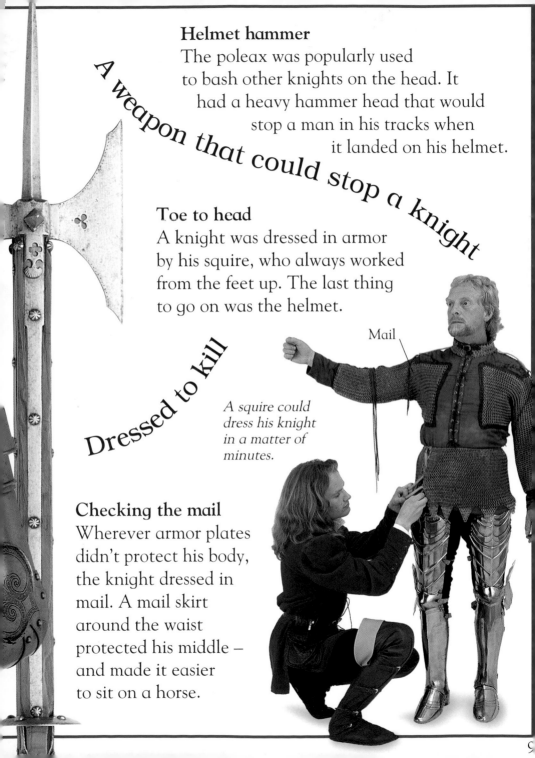

Helmet hammer
The poleax was popularly used
to bash other knights on the head. It
had a heavy hammer head that would
stop a man in his tracks when
it landed on his helmet.

A weapon that could stop a knight

Toe to head
A knight was dressed in armor
by his squire, who always worked
from the feet up. The last thing
to go on was the helmet.

Mail

Dressed to kill

*A squire could
dress his knight
in a matter of
minutes.*

Checking the mail
Wherever armor plates
didn't protect his body,
the knight dressed in
mail. A mail skirt
around the waist
protected his middle –
and made it easier
to sit on a horse.

Castle comfort.

Castles were like village housing the lord's fam servants, soldiers, and priests. People gathe in the Great Hall for meals and to watch the day's business.

A servant draws yarn from a spinning wheel.

Evenings were spent without television –

Board games

Board games such as checkers and backgammon were popular. Chess was a favorite because it had a mock battlefield where pieces could attack and capture each other.

Children play an old board game called "Foxes and Geese."

g with food
j the evening
musicians
mes played
rtain. After
ests had
they began
ce.

le enjoyed

A hornpipe was a popular choice of instrument for a 15th-century musician.

live music, games, and dance.

Marriage

Noble women married young – some at the age of 14! Marriages were arranged to increase power and wealth.

A busy life

A lady of the castle was supposed to spin wool and sew, and run the kitchens and living quarters. She also had to receive and entertain guests, and take charge of running the castle if her husband was away.

ueen of the castle

Dining and hunting

A castle's kitchen was a busy place. The "stove" was a huge open fireplace where meat was roasted and bread was baked in special ovens. Then servants ferried the dishes to the Great Hall.

Feast your eyes
Banquets were gra
affairs with elaborat
platters of roast boar
baked fish, and
spicy pastries.

Flat pieces of stale bread were used as pla

Most fresh fruits and vegetables came from the castle gardens.

for fun
nobles loved to go
king" – hunting with
s or falcons. It took
skill to train a wild
o kill and
eturn to
ster.

Hood

Bird blinders
The only way to
keep a falcon from
attacking every
time it saw other
birds was to blindfold it
with a tiny hood. Just
before being let loose,
the hood was slipped off.

Not a glove puppet
A hawk handler wore thick
leather gloves to prevent a hawk's
sharp talons from cutting
his hand.

rained killer

Essential clothing

*Short leather
thongs, called jesses,
were fastened to the
bird's legs to keep
it perched on a fist.*

*Tough leather
glove*

The castle killers

There are three ways to capture a castle: Demanding its surrender without a fight is the fastest. Starving out the defenders is the slowest. Battering down the walls with special machines is the hardest.

Slinging the shot

Heavy shot
A large trebuchet worked like a giant slingshot, flinging stones that weighed as much as a man up to 980 ft (300 m).

Traction trebuchet

Making a rock fly
A team of men were needed to yank the of a small trebuchet giving its short end sharp tug. The lon and sling would th swing up swiftly hurl a rock forw

The aim wasn't accurate, but wh the rock hit its target it did a lot of damage

LIBRARY
ANDERSON ELEMENTARY SCHOOL

Twaaang!

The catapult had a short wooden arm with a cup at one end that could fling rocks, dead animals, flaming rags, and any other missiles that might make life miserable for the defenders.

Tunneling in

If a castle had no moat, attackers sometimes dug their way in under the walls – or they dug deep enough to make the walls collapse.

Catapult

Seige towers could scale the castle walls.

Defenders had a good view of the enemy's movements from the turrets.

Hard hats

In displays of skill or battles to the death, armor shielded a knight from danger. But it could get very hot under his heavy helmet!

The German
this h
"Hund"
(hound's

B

Eye slit

Jousting
helmet
1400s

The helm was t

Cras
This helm
over 16 lbs (7.4 kg)
strapped to the body
so the knight's sh
bore the incredible

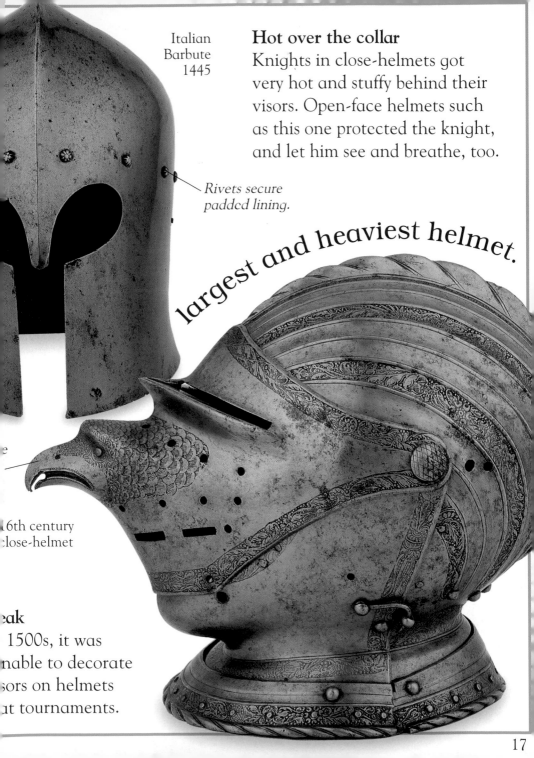

Italian
Barbute
1445

Hot over the collar
Knights in close-helmets got
very hot and stuffy behind their
visors. Open-face helmets such
as this one protected the knight,
and let him see and breathe, too.

*Rivets secure
padded lining.*

largest and heaviest helmet.

6th century
close-helmet

eak

1500s, it was
nable to decorate
sors on helmets
t tournaments.

17

Flashing blades

Knights used swords. A big two-edged cutt
sword was wielded by slashing it from side
side. Pointed swords could
be stabbed into the joints
in an opponent's armor.

The sword

Ceremonial
sword

Scottish claymore

Highlander two-hander!
This two-handed Scottish claymore
was made around 1620, and
used in the Scottish highlands.
"Claymore" means "great sword."

sword could cut

Two-handed sword

The two-handed

Lugs prevente
enemy weapo
from sliding d
the blade.

stab wounds

...n holy men were not
...osed to carry
...tional weapons, so
...ad this dagger blade
...hidden inside a
...ing stick.

Indian steel dagger

*Scroll handle has
a lotus flower tip.*

...s the most important knightly weapon.

*This two-handed sword
was probably
used in
ceremonies.*

g arm methods

...ers had to be strong to swing two-
...ed swords. They were the biggest
...ls used and packed a terrific punch.

Cutting
sword

gh mail and bone!

pike slicer

...sword was made with a wavy
...to lop off the heads of long
...carried by foot soldiers.

*Single-edged
sword*

Bows and arro

Mounted soldiers feared attac
from foot soldiers armed with longl
and crossbows. Swift arrows could l
down horses and pierce the
thickest armor.

Guns were not as pc
as crossbov
the

Power of the bow

A 14th-century crossbow was
so powerful it could kill
a man at 650 ft
(200 m).

Crossbows were slow to load

but easy to sl

*This bow was
so strong, it had to
be loaded with
a crank.*

*A steel tipped
bolt for war*

*The arrow
(called a bolt)
fitted in this
groove.*

*A wide-headed
bolt for hunting*

Bolt from the blue

When a steel-tipped bolt
from a crossbow hit iron armor
straight on and at close range, it
could punch a hole right through it.

of practice
k years of
ice to fire
gbow well.
t strength
eeded
nage
of
st
s
g).

A longbow was as tall as an archer.

Arrow shafts were
made from birch or
ash wood. The flights
were goose feathers.

Longbows were
carved from a
single piece
of wood.

of death
d longbowmen
d fire 12 arrows
ute, sending a
of arrows through the air. Their biggest
em was running out of arrows during a battle.

Riding to war

A knight needed a horse to ride into battle, as well as for hunting, jousting, and carting all of his possessions. Most knights had several horses.

Most knights could only afford head armor

Proud steed

This 16th-century horse armor was made to protect a horse's head and neck. The metal has been decorated with etchir of birds and animals.

15th-century rowel spur

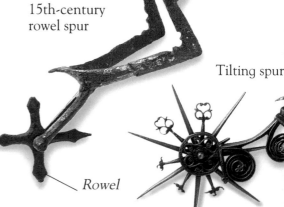

Tilting spur

Spurred on

Jousting knights had spurs with a rotating spiked wheel or rowel to urge their horses to charge each other.

Rowel

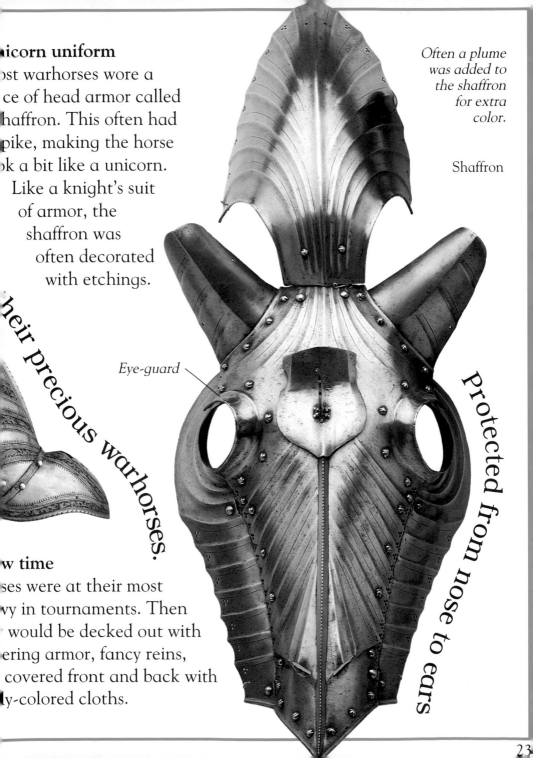

icorn uniform

)st warhorses wore a
ce of head armor called
haffron. This often had
pike, making the horse
)k a bit like a unicorn.
Like a knight's suit
of armor, the
shaffron was
often decorated
with etchings.

*Often a plume
was added to
the shaffron
for extra
color.*

Shaffron

heir precious warhorses.

Eye-guard

Protected from nose to ears

w time

ses were at their most
vy in tournaments. Then
would be decked out with
ering armor, fancy reins,
covered front and back with
ly-colored cloths.

23

Lance a lot

In the 1200s, mock battles, or tourneys, we
fought between teams on horseback. The
highlight was a
joust – a battle
between two
mounted
knights.

a blunted lance

A knight used

Clash o
The k
clas
heavi
som
the horse
knocked

ilt
e 1400s, barriers called tilts
set up to stop the charging
s from colliding. Special
armor protected
nights.

Family colors
Each knight had his own family
crest marked on his shield,
his tunic, and even on the
cloth covering his horse.
This was known as
a coat of arms.

try to push his opponent to the ground.

Wooden lances
splintered
easily on impact.

e
the knights
dismount
ontinue the
with swords.

at a tournament

Staying alive

A suit of armor protected a knight from head to toe.

Heavy head

A helmet usually weighed between 3 to 7 lbs (1½ to 3 kg). It was lined for comfort and had a chin strap to keep it from flying off in battle.

A shell fit to take serious punishment.

Movable visor

Collar plate to protect the neck.

Plated armor around waist allowed easy movement

Shoulder armor fitted over the breast and back plates.

Elbow guard

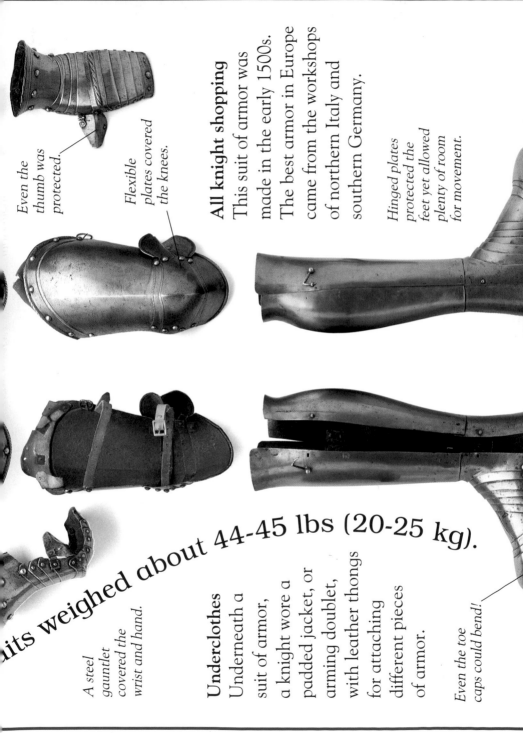

Even the thumb was protected.

Flexible plates covered the knees.

All knight shopping

This suit of armor was made in the early 1500s. The best armor in Europe came from the workshops of northern Italy and southern Germany.

Hinged plates protected the feet yet allowed plenty of room for movement.

...its weighed about 44-45 lbs (20-25 kg).

A steel gauntlet covered the wrist and hand.

Underclothes

Underneath a suit of armor, a knight wore a padded jacket, or arming doublet, with leather thongs for attaching different pieces of armor.

Even the toe caps could bend!

World at war

Many ingenious weapons have appeared around the world. These deadly axes and vicious blades prove that there was no lack of imagination when it came to inventing weird weapons of war.

Tiger claw

Not even safe to shake hands
Tigers in India gave local people a gruesome idea for this hand weapon called a tiger claw.

Not one to throw away
This African throwing knife from Zaire spun as it flew. No matter which side hit, it was bound to do a lot of damage.

Iron blade

Throwing knife

Leather and copper binding

Cruel and gruesor

p, hack, slash

Covered cutting edge

Armed arms
This circular wrist knife was worn in
Kenya. The razor-sharp edge is covered
to make it safer to handle.

weapons from around the world.

One spike always points upward.

Caltrop

Don't drop that caltrop
Caltrops, or crow's feet, were
four-pointed spikes that were
thrown on the ground to
cripple charging horses.

Three spikes rest on the ground.

Index

Five chivalrous questions

1) On what level was the door to

2) What kind of skirts did knights

3) Who was in charge of a castle knight was away?

4) What was a knight doing if he "hawking?"

5) What kind of slingshot could k down castle walls?

  (a) a rockenroll
  (b) a catapult
  (c) a gondola
  (d) a trebuchet
  (e) a flingula

Answers on page 32

Who would have lived in a place like this?

Answers

From page 30: 1. The door was on the second floor

2. Mail armor skirts around the middle

3. The lady of the castle

4. Hunting with a hawk or falcon

5. A trebuchet

From page 31: A German lord lived in this castle along the Rhine River during the Middle Ages. From here he commanded a great stretch of river.

Anderson Elementary School

105155085   940.1 MAY

Incredible castles and knights

DATE DUE
